ELLIOTT CARTER

FIGMENT V

for Solo Marimba

HENDON MUSIC

BOOSEY & HAWKES

AN IMAGEM COMPANY

DISTRIBUTED BY

HAL•LEONARD®
CORPORATION
7777 W. BLUEMOUND RD. P.O. BOX 13819 MILWAUKEE, WI 53213

www.boosey.com
www.halleonard.com

Published by Hendon Music, Inc.
A Boosey & Hawkes company
229 West 28th Street, 11th Fl
New York NY 10001

www. boosey.com

Music engraving by Thomas Brodhead

First performed on 2 May 2009
at the Frederick Loewe Theater, New York University, New York, NY
by Simon Boyar, marimba

PROGRAM NOTE

This Figment for marimba solo was written in February 2009, as a present for the 17th birthday of my dear grandson Alexander, who is interested in percussion instruments.

—Elliott Carter

ANMERKUNGEN DES KOMPONISTEN

Dieses *Figment* für Marimbaphon solo wurde im Februar 2009 als Geschenk zum 17. Geburtstag meines Enkels Alexander verfasst, da er sich sehr für Schlaginstrumente interessiert.

—Elliott Carter

COMMENTAIRE DU COMPOSITEUR

Cette pièce pour marimba seul a été composée en février 2009 comme cadeau pour le 17ème anniversaire de mon petit-fils Alexander, qui s'intéresse beaucoup aux instruments à percussion.

—Elliott Carter

PERFORMANCE SUGGESTION

Use medium-hard yarn mallets.

Duration: 2 minutes

for Alexander

FIGMENT V

for Solo Marimba

Elliott Carter
(2009)

* All notes marked staccato should be played as dead strokes, in order to clearly
define the difference between staccato and non-staccato notes.

979–0–051–10660–8

* May be played with two mallets.

Feb. 3, 2009, NYC

MICHAEL DAUGHERTY

SING SING: J. EDGAR HOOVER

FOR STRING QUARTET AND PRE-RECORDED SOUND
(1992)

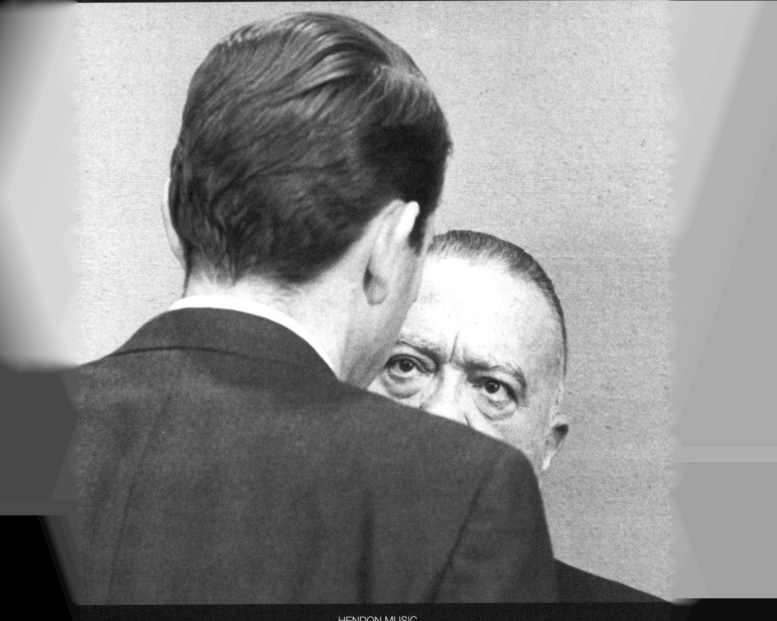

HENDON MUSIC

BOOSEY & HAWKES

AN IMAGEM COMPANY

DISTRIBUTED BY

HAL•LEONARD®
CORPORATION
7777 W. BLUEMOUND RD. P.O. BOX 13819 MILWAUKEE, WI 53213

www.boosey.com
www.halleonard.com

Published by Hendon Music, Inc.
a Boosey & Hawkes company
229 West 28th Street, 11th Floor
New York NY 10001

www.boosey.com

 AN IMAGEM COMPANY

Photography:
Yoichi Okamoto, *J. Edgar Hoover* (1967)
LBJ Library, University of Texas, Austin, Texas
Used by Permission

ISMN 979-0-051-09694-7 for score alone; 979-0-051-10599-1 for score and parts

First printed 2012
Printed and distributed by Hal Leonard Corporation, Milwaukee WI
Engraving by Peter Simcich

Commissioned by Kronos Quartet
David Harrington and John Sherba, violins, Hank Dutt, viola and Joan Jeanrenaud, cello

First performed by Kronos Quartet at the Vic Theatre
on January 23, 1993 in Chicago, Illinois

First recorded by Kronos Quartet on "Howl, U.S.A"
Nonesuch 7559-79372-2

BIOGRAPHY

Michael Daugherty is one of the most commissioned, performed, and recorded composers on the American concert music scene today. His music is rich with cultural allusions and bears the stamp of classic modernism, with colliding tonalities and blocks of sound; at the same time, his melodies can be eloquent and stirring. Daugherty has been hailed by *The Times* (London) as "a master icon maker" with a "maverick imagination, fearless structural sense and meticulous ear." Daugherty first came to international attention when the Baltimore Symphony Orchestra, conducted by David Zinman, performed his *Metropolis Symphony* at Carnegie Hall in 1994. Since that time, Daugherty's music has entered the orchestral, band and chamber music repertory and made him, according to the League of American Orchestras, one of the ten most performed American composers.

In 2011, the Nashville Symphony's Naxos recording of Daugherty's *Metropolis Symphony* and *Deus ex Machina* was honored with three GRAMMY® Awards, including Best Classical Contemporary Composition.

Born in 1954 in Cedar Rapids, Iowa, Daugherty is the son of a dance-band drummer and the oldest of five brothers, all professional musicians. He studied music composition at the University of North Texas (1972-76), the Manhattan School of Music (1976-78), and computer music at Pierre Boulez's IRCAM in Paris (1979-80). Daugherty received his doctorate from Yale University in 1986 where his teachers included Jacob Druckman, Earle Brown, Roger Reynolds, and Bernard Rands. During this time, he also collaborated with jazz arranger Gil Evans in New York, and pursued further studies with composer György Ligeti in Hamburg, Germany (1982-84). After teaching music composition from 1986-90 at the Oberlin Conservatory of Music, Daugherty joined the School of Music at the University of Michigan (Ann Arbor) in 1991, where he is Professor of Composition and a mentor to many of today's most talented young composers.

Daugherty has been Composer-in-Residence with the Louisville Symphony Orchestra (2000), Detroit Symphony Orchestra (1999-2003), Colorado Symphony Orchestra (2001-02), Cabrillo Festival of Contemporary Music (2001-04, 2006-08, 2011), Westshore Symphony Orchestra (2005-06), Eugene Symphony (2006), the Henry Mancini Summer Institute (2006), the Music from Angel Fire Chamber Music Festival (2006), and the Pacific Symphony (2010).

Daugherty has received numerous awards, distinctions, and fellowships for his music, including: a Fulbright Fellowship (1977), the Kennedy Center Friedheim Award (1989), the Goddard Lieberson Fellowship from the American Academy of Arts and Letters (1991), fellowships from the National Endowment for the Art (1992) and the Guggenheim Foundation (1996), and the Stoeger Prize from the Chamber Music Society of Lincoln Center (2000). In 2005, Daugherty received the Lancaster Symphony Orchestra Composer's Award, and in 2007, the Delaware Symphony Orchestra selected Daugherty as the winner of the A.I. DuPont Award. Also in 2007, he received the American Bandmasters Association Ostwald Award for his composition *Raise the Roof* for Timpani and Symphonic Band. Daugherty has been named "Outstanding Classical Composer" at the Detroit Music Awards in 2007, 2009 and 2010. His GRAMMY® award winning recordings can be heard on Albany, Argo, Delos, Equilibrium, Klavier, Naxos and Nonesuch labels.

J. Edgar Hoover, Director of the FBI from 1932-72, in the Oval Office of the White House (1967)

Sing Sing: J. Edgar Hoover for string quartet and pre-recorded sound was commissioned by Kronos Quartet. The first performance was given by Kronos Quartet in Chicago, Illinois at the Vic Theatre on January 23, 1993. My composition is about the man who directed the U.S. Federal Bureau of Investigation virtually unchallenged from 1924 until his death in 1972.

My composition opens with one of J. Edgar Hoover's favorite mottoes: "The FBI is as close to you as your nearest telephone." This "reassurance" to the American public also served to authorize his systematic invasion of their privacy: for Hoover, the telephone became an instrument for playing out his lifetime obsession with collecting sensitive information for his so-called "secret files." Throughout his 48 years as director of the FBI, Hoover ordered the wiretapping of the telephones of movies stars, gangsters, presidents, civil rights activists, politicians, communist sympathizers, entertainers, and anyone who opposed his own political and moral agenda.

For me, the motto offers an opportunity to listen in on Hoover's voice, and to manipulate it for my own compositional purposes. The telephone, like the digital technology I have used, mediates voice so that it is both distant and near. I wanted to bring the dead voice of J. Edgar Hoover back to a posthumous life through technology, so that it may "sing" of its own death. I created the tape part by digitally sampling bits of actual historical speeches delivered by Hoover from 1941 to 1972, to such diverse audiences as the American Legion, Boys' Club of America, and the FBI National Academy.

It was eerie to be the first person to hear these tapes since they were made available to the public. I composed string parts to "sing along" with Hoover, in order to convey my sense of Hoover's grim, threatening, yet darkly comic personality. The part played by the string quartet is also inspired by sounds associated with the FBI, such as sirens, American patriotic songs, and machine gun syncopations. The quartet therefore creates another context for hearing Hoover's own words: "I hope that this presentation will serve to give you a better knowledge and a deeper understanding of YOUR FBI."

—Michael Daugherty

Recordings obtained from the J. Edgar Hoover F.B.I tapes at the National Archives in
Washington, D.C. through the Freedom of Information Act.

We are as close to you as your telephone

J. Edgar Hoover:

I hope that this presentation will serve to give you a better
knowledge and deeper understanding of your F.B.I.
We are as close to you as your telephone.

Get your hands up!

F.B.I Agent:

F.B.I.! Get your hands up! The charge is murder!

Look at your watch

J. Edgar Hoover:

Look at your watch this morning
as it ticks off twelve seconds–
A murder every forty-six seconds...
there is a burglary or assault to kill each seven minutes, a robbery–
Every hour a major crime has been committed somewhere in these United States–
another serious crime is added to the nation's total.

The growing menace of communism

Radio Announcer:

The growing menace of communism arouses the House of Representatives Un-American
Activities Committee. Among the well-informed witnesses testifying is J. Edgar Hoover,
head of the Federal Bureau of Investigation. Mr. Hoover speaks with authority on the subject.

J. Edgar Hoover:

Communism / The enemy / Nikita Khrushchev / Deadly menace /
Communists and their dupes / play it dirty or you're not a communist /
Atheistic communism / enemy of the American people /
I thank you.

Personnages à longues Oreilles

J. Edgar Hoover:

The F.B.I: Fidelity, Bravery and Integrity.
The world is witnessing a giant ideological battle. A battle for the hearts, minds, and souls
of men, women, and children. The communists desire to destroy our cherished liberties and
establish a dictatorship. They are working to make this nation part of a world communist empire.
This is the danger which we face today. The time has come for Americans to wake-up!
We can, and will, win this battle. The stakes are high. We cannot afford to lose. If the communists
take control, our entire civilization will be destroyed and mankind will be rolled back to
barbarism.
Very often the question is asked, "What can I, as one citizen, do to defeat communism?"
My answer is that you can do a lot.

Keep it a secret

J. Edgar Hoover:

Keep it a secret / Open the files of the F.B.I.

The land of the free...

Brainwashed /

and the home of the brave...

the American people / Abraham Lincoln / moral decay / they zig and zag / Reds!
Mobsters! / Parasites! / President Kennedy / moral decay / Dread swastika of the Nazis /
America / Keep it a secret

Open the files of the FBI / Keep it a secret /

The greatest concentration of communist workers have been found in three fields in
the United States...

in education, unions and entertainment. It is disheartening that more young people appear
to know the words of popular soap jingles than the meaningful words of the "Star-Spangled
Banner."

Star-Spangled Banner

J. Edgar Hoover and crowd at American Legion convention (ca. 1963):

Oh, say can you see...

Fear silences the voice /

What so proudly we hailed...

Fear silences the voices of protest /

Whose broad stripes and bright stars...

O'er the ramparts we watched...

Fear silences the voices of protest /

And the rockets' red glare...

There is no place in America for vigilantes, rabble rousers, the lunatic fringe /

Gave proof through the night that our flag was still there...

Oh, say does that star-spangled banner yet wave...

Fear silences the voice of our society /

Home of the brave...

Fear

J. Edgar Hoover:

Fear silences the voice /

Ladies and Gentlemen

we cannot afford to lose.

There can be no compromise.

The F.B.I.

"He can't get away with it!"

I thank you.

PERFORMANCE NOTE

If performing *Sing Sing J. Edgar Hoover* in a large performance space, it is recommended to amplify the string quartet. Each individual player should be amplified with a microphone, preferably with a lavalier-style microphone attached to each string instrument. If this is not possible, then the string quartet may be amplified utilizing conventional air microphones or pick-ups. To get maximum pickup with a minimum chance of feedback, air microphones should be placed within a few inches of each string instrument *f* hole. A six-channel mixer and house and monitor speakers are recommended for performance: 4 channels for the string quartet and two channels for the electronic device playing back the pre-recorded sound. A sound technician with a good musical ear is necessary during performance so that the string quartet and pre-recorded sound are balanced and clearly heard by the audience.

If performing *Sing Sing J. Edgar Hoover* in a small performance space, the string quartet may perform without amplification. Small speakers for playback of the pre-recorded sound are recommended. The speakers should be placed slightly behind the string quartet so they serve both as house and monitor speakers. The playback volume of the pre-recorded sound should be adjusted so that the string quartet and pre-recorded sound are balanced and clearly heard by the audience throughout the performance.

A stereo CD, which contains the pre-recorded sound that is necessary for performance, is included with the published score. Cues for rehearsal and performance are listed below:

CUES FOR REHEARSAL AND PERFORMANCE

CD Track List of pre-recorded sound

1. Measure 1 – Letter E: We are as close to you as your telephone
2. Letter F: Get your hands up!
3. Letter G: Look at your watch
4. Letter H: The growing menace of Communism
5. Letter I: Personnages à longues oreilles
6. Letter J: Keep it a secret
7. Letter L: Star-Spangled Banner
8. Letter M: Fear

STAGE ARRANGEMENT
(when using amplification)

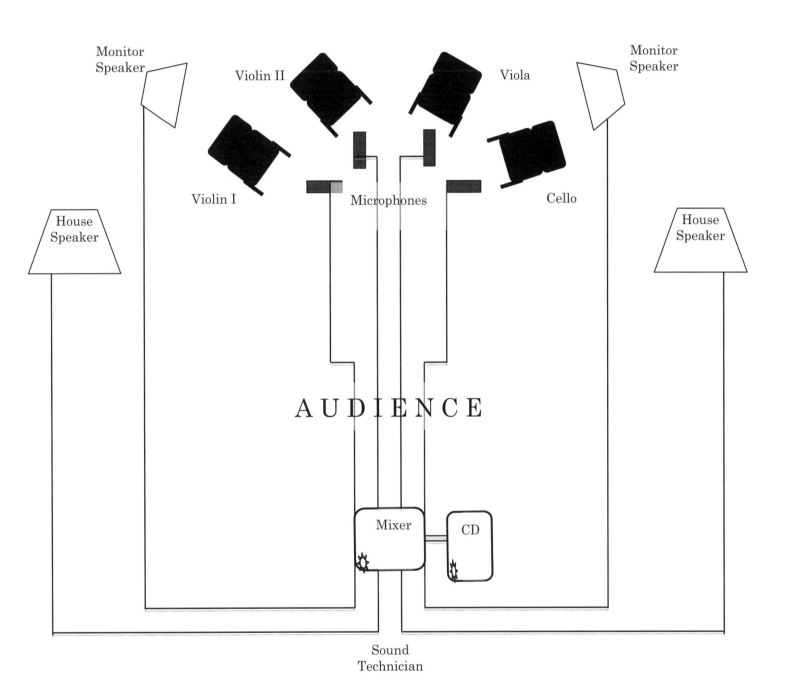

Monitor Speaker

Violin II

Viola

Monitor Speaker

House Speaker

Violin I

Microphones

Cello

House Speaker

AUDIENCE

Mixer

CD

Sound Technician

INSTRUMENTATION

Pre-recorded sound

Violin I
Violin II
Viola
Cello

Duration: 11 minutes

Sing Sing: J. Edgar Hoover

for String Quartet and pre-recorded sound

Michael Daugherty (1992)
(revised by composer 2011)

ISMN 979-0-051-09694-7

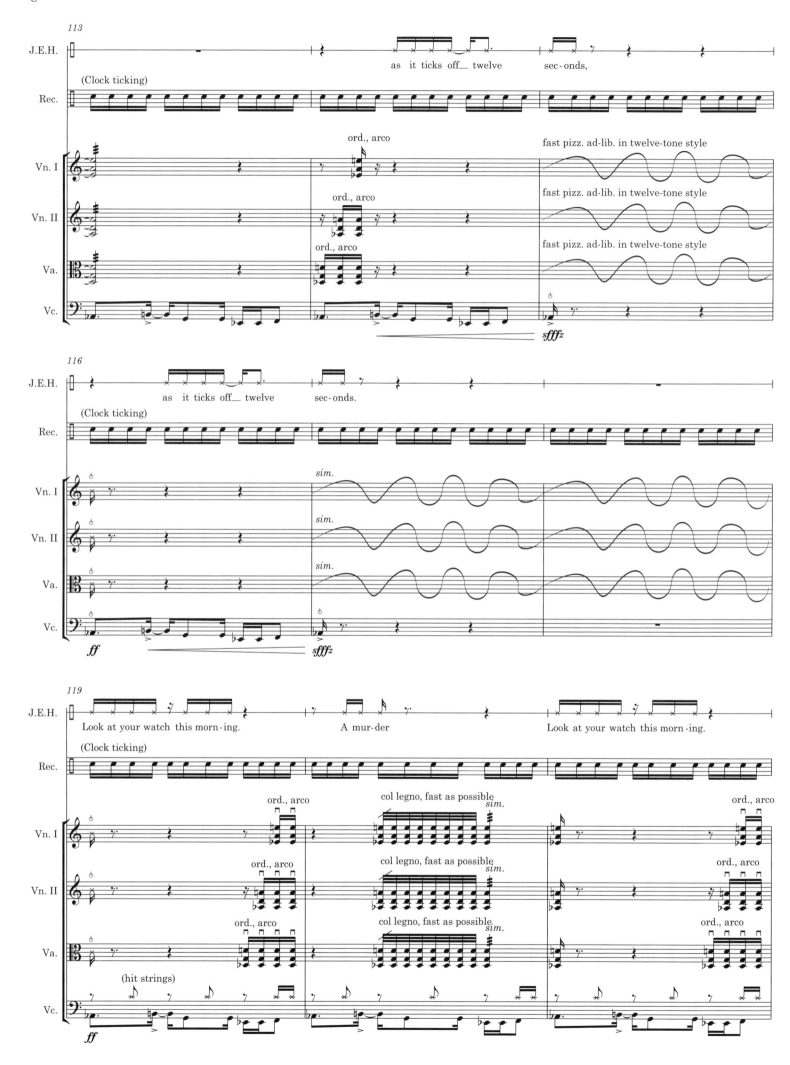

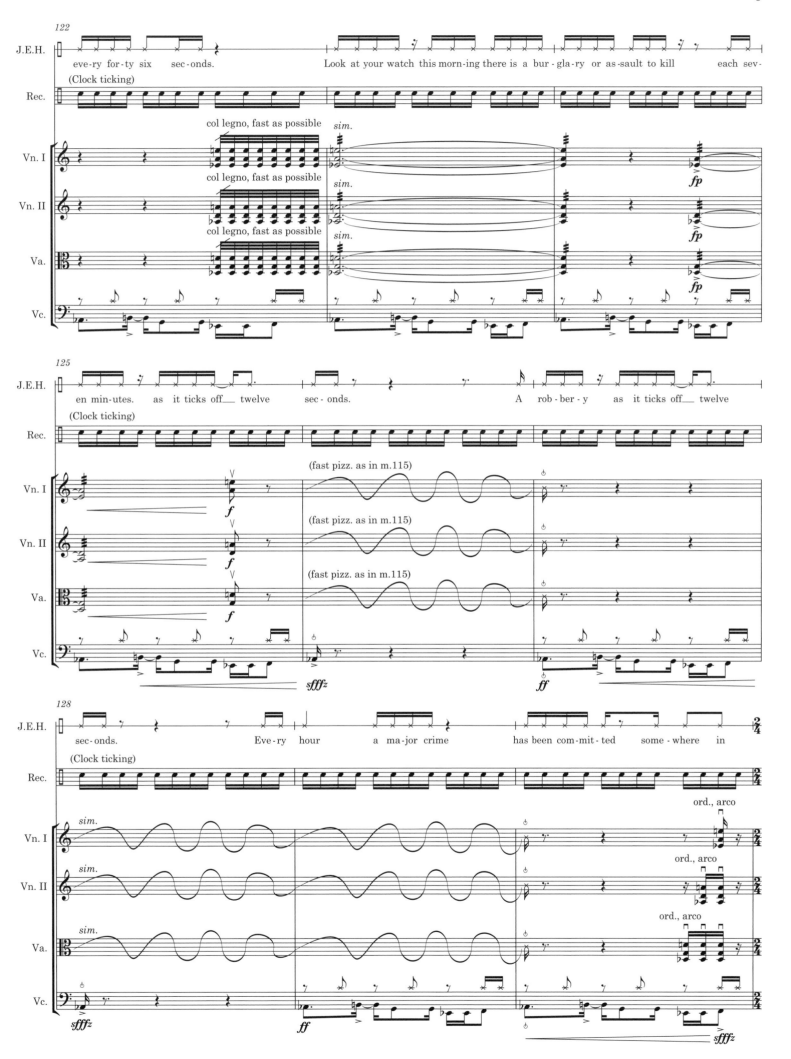

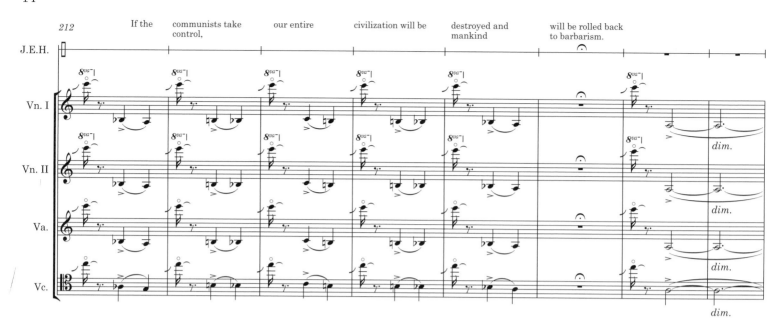

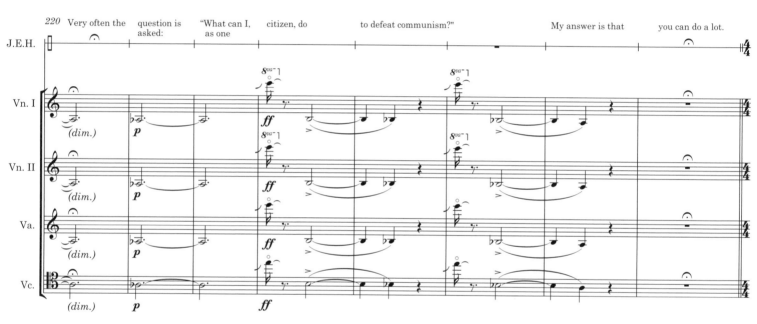

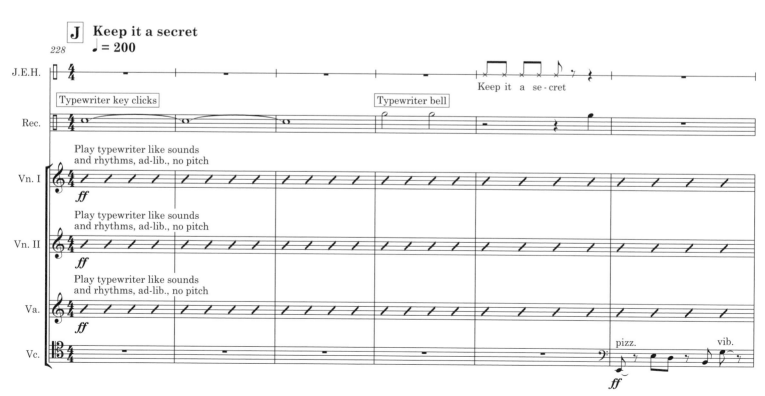